THE

BEARDSTOWN
LADIES'

Little Book of Investment Wisdom

THE

BEARDSTOWN

LADIES'

Little Book of Investment Wisdom

A SETH GODIN PRODUCTION

THE BEARDSTOWN LADIES'
INVESTMENT CLUB

Edited by

Robin Dellabough

HYPERION
New York

Copyright © 1997 The Beardstown Ladies' Investment Club

All photos courtesy of the Beardstown Ladies.
Illustrations copyright 1997 © Hal Just.

Printed in the United States of America.
For information address
Hyperion, 114 Fifth Avenue, New York, New York 10011

Library of Congress Cataloging-in-Publication Data
The Beardstown Ladies' little book of investment wisdom /
The Beardstown Ladies' Investment Club ;
edited by Robin Dellabough.
p. cm. ISBN 0-7868-6373-0
1. Investments—United States—Handbooks, manuals, etc.
2. Saving and investments—United States—Handbooks, manuals, etc.
3. Investment clubs—United States—Handbooks, manuals, etc
I. Dellabough, Robin. II. Beardstown Ladies' Investment Club.
HG4527.B373 1997
332.6—dc21 97–21505
CIP

Designed by Nicola Ferguson
First Edition

1 3 5 7 9 10 8 6 4 2

We dedicate this book to our families. Their love has

supported us as we continue to share a portion

of our lives with you, our readers.

—THE BEARDSTOWN LADIES

CONTENTS

ACKNOWLEDGMENTS

FROM THE BEARDSTOWN LADIES:

Thanks to the Beardstown Chamber of Commerce and Donna Strieker for continued support. They have shipped our video and books throughout the world and answer numerous inquiries regarding our guest nights and other matters.

Thanks to our employers who have supported our decision to share our knowledge with others. They have willingly given us the time away from work when needed.

Thanks to all the new friends that we have made across the country and abroad. Your warm receptions have reinforced our incentive to continue to share, and to say, "If we can do this, you can too!"

FROM THE EDITOR:

At Hyperion

Thanks to Laurie Abkemeier and Brian DeFiore for grace under pressure and pressuring with grace.

At Seth Godin Productions

Thanks to Lisa DiMona, Seth Godin, Julie Maner, Sarah Silbert, Nana Sledzieski, and Karen Watts for their own special brand of wit and wisdom.

SPECIAL THANKS:

We wish to thank Keith Colter and Carolyn Patterson of Central Picture Entertainment, Inc., who created the award-winning video production, "Cookin' Up Profits on Wall Street."

THE BEARDSTOWN LADIES' INVESTMENT CLUB

Ann Brewer, 64, secretary, charter member.

Ann Corley, 69, retired homemaker, member since 1985.

Doris Edwards, 78, elementary school principal, charter member.

Sylvia Gaushell, 86, retired art teacher, member since 1991.

Shirley Gross, 80, retired medical technologist, charter member.

Margaret Houchins, 56, former gift and flower shop owner, member since 1991.

Ruth Huston, 78, retired owner of a dry-cleaning business, charter member.

CARNELL KORSMEYER, 70, hog farm owner, past president of the National Pork Board, charter member.

HAZEL LINDAHL, 90, retired medical technician and school nurse, charter member.

CAROL MCCOMBS, 48, insurance agent, Elsie Scheer's daughter, member since 1993.

ELSIE SCHEER, 80, retired farmer and teacher's aide, charter member.

BETTY SINNOCK, 65, bank trust officer, charter member.

MAXINE THOMAS, 76, retired bank officer, charter member.

BUFFY TILLITT-PRATT, 44, real estate broker, member since 1987.

THE

BEARDSTOWN

LADIES'

Little Book of Investment Wisdom

INTRODUCTION

When we started our investment club fourteen years ago, our main goal was to learn as much as we could. Little by little, we educated ourselves about the stock market and how to invest. As the months and meetings rolled by, we found we were learning even more than we had expected. Soon people outside the club began asking us questions, and we gained some recognition for doing pretty well with our small investments. Then we were approached by publishers to write a book based on our experiences. We did, and *The Beardstown Ladies' Common-Sense Investment Guide* proved to be of interest to a lot of readers. As we promoted our book, people asked us questions about how to start saving money and where to find the money to invest. To answer those questions, we wrote two more books: *The Beardstown Ladies' Stitch-in-Time Guide to Growing Your Nest Egg* and *The Beardstown Ladies' Guide to Smart Spending for Big Savings*. We have been both pleased and amazed at the interest in managing money and investing that our books have sparked. Many of our readers have taken the time to tell us that we have been an inspiration and that's the fuel that has kept us going. We've found that sharing our knowledge, through both our mistakes and our successes, has given each of us another opportunity to learn even more.

We never anticipated that by focusing on learning, we'd wind up sharing that information with others. But these days, that's really what seems most important about our investment club. We continue to learn and to improve our investment portfolio so that our club may serve as a useful model. We have open meetings three times a year so that visitors can observe how we structure our meetings and do our homework on the companies we choose to buy. We are so pleased that our down-to-earth approach is of value to people. Our goal today is to continue educating ourselves and others. We know that it isn't possible for everyone to visit us, so this little book is another way of saying, "You can do it too!"

We've combed through all of our combined experience to come up with what we believe to be our most essential pearls of wisdom. We looked toward our past ("As Aunt Margaret used to say") as well as our future ("Bless our computers") in - compiling this book. Some of these maxims are ideas we've picked up from the "experts" over the years, presented here with our own Beardstown interpretation. Some grew out of our unique situation. Some are investment rules, while others are rules to live by.

In the end, we realized we were really creating a kind of "scrapbook" for our family of readers. Just as a page in a scrapbook is a visual reminder of a whole party or an entire vacation or a new chapter in one's life, each of these epigrams is a shortened version of good, solid information. Instead of a summary stew of our previous books, this volume is like the icing on the cake. Every one of these ideas has worked for us and we think they will work for you too.

We hope that by browsing through our album, you will be inspired to invest wisely and well.

FINANCIAL
PLANNING

ON A RIVER
THERE IS NO
STANDING STILL.

On a river you can't just do nothing because that river will take you somewhere and it may not be where you want to go. So it is with life—if you don't have a plan you may find yourself where you don't want to be.

WE LIVE BY
THE THREE E'S.

Education, enjoyment, and enrichment were the three goals set by our club in the beginning. We stand by them today and think they also apply to others. We know that they have been good for us.

YOU HAVE TO TAKE STOCK
TO BUY STOCK.

efore you can decide how much or where to invest, you need to assess your own financial picture. What is your current financial situation? How much money do you want to save and when do you need it? Only by answering these questions can you evaluate your best investment strategy.

HOPE FOR THE BEST, BUT BE PREPARED FOR THE WORST.

*T*hat's what Aunt Margaret used to say. It's the reason we believe in thorough financial planning. We want to be prepared for whatever may come our way.

FEAR OF INVESTING
IS LIKE FEAR
OF FLYING.

*I*t can be overcome. As Elsie says, "If I always do what I've always done, I'll always get what I've always got."

18

TURN STUMBLING BLOCKS
INTO STEPPING-STONES.

*W*e can't predict our future, but making the most of what life throws our way will help to ensure a more comfortable one.

20

MAKE SURE EVERYONE DOESN'T SIT IN THE SAME END OF THE CANOE.

*J*ust as we wouldn't want everyone to sit in the same end of the canoe, we do not want all of our money in one investment. We want to diversify, and we may have to rebalance our investments to maintain our original allocations.

AFTER YOU GO LILY PADDING, TRY YELLOW PADDING.

Two sisters used to float in a boat on a pond filled with waterlilies, talking and dreaming about what they'd be like when they grew up. Now that they're adults, they use the phrase "lily padding" to mean that sort of easygoing planning. So start your financial planning by daydreaming. Then when you're ready, you can write things down on a legal pad or notebook or whatever you prefer.

24

IF YOU GET RICH QUICK, YOU'LL PROBABLY GET POOR EVEN QUICKER.

*I*f an investment seems too good to be true, it probably is. Don't fall prey to get-rich-quick schemes. Stick with those time-proven ways to grow your nest egg.

DON'T LOSE SLEEP TO GAIN MONEY.

Each individual must weigh carefully how much investment risk he or she is willing to take. If you're losing sleep worrying over your investments, they're not worth the possible return, no matter how high. Life is too short.

HISTORY IS A GOOD
TEACHER.

earn from the past, live for the present,
and plan for the future.

INVESTING IS AS EASY AS
APPLE PIE.

Well, that's what the Beardstown Ladies think. Just as we follow a recipe when we are in the kitchen, we do our homework when we are searching for stock investments. We think that using a disciplined approach in the kitchen and in investing will bring successful results!

TEAMWORK HELPS BEAT
THE CLOCK.

*I*t's amazing what you can accomplish when you're working as a team. By sharing the workload we can all learn much more in far less time than when we are left to do it alone. Shirley says that the investment club is doing her homework for her now and that's how we all feel.

SAVING
MONEY

PAY YOURSELF FIRST.

nn Brewer is a strong believer in this savings concept. Every pay period, pay yourself before you pay your regular bills. It may not be much, but, getting into the habit of investing in yourself is much more important than the amount.

STOP AND CONSIDER.

*B*efore you buy anything, ask: Can you really afford it? Is it the best value for the money? Are there other things you'd rather spend money on? How will you feel about the purchase tomorrow?

SPENDING AND SAVING
THE BEARDSTOWN WAY
IS NOT A HOBBY.

*I*t's an overall attitude toward money. It's a way of looking at your life, and figuring out where things fit into it and what really matters to you, rather than simply spending for pleasure or to entertain yourself. If you train yourself to continually spend less than you earn and invest the difference, your future will be much more secure.

A FOOL AND HIS MONEY
ARE SOON PARTED.

 Beardstown Lady and her money are soon invested.

MIND YOUR
P'S AND Q'S.

ylvia tells us to pay our fair share but nothing more.

STATEMENTS AREN'T
ALWAYS RIGHT.

Checking all your statements thoroughly and questioning those items that don't look right to you could save you dollars. It pays to question.

LISTEN TO YOURSELF.

*Y*ou usually know exactly what you should be spending, or what you should be doing to save money. If you listen to yourself, it's easier not to let your emotions get the better of you. Ask yourself, "Do I really need that?" or "Can I save that money?"

FOCUS ON THE BIG-TICKET ITEMS AND THE LITTLE THINGS WILL TAKE CARE OF THEMSELVES.

*P*eople ask us how we find money to invest. We simply try to spend our money only on what matters. We take the time to educate ourselves before we go to make the big dollar purchases. This has resulted in savings of hundreds, even thousands of dollars that can be invested or used elsewhere.

DON'T LET THE MAGIC OF COMPOUND INTEREST TURN INTO A CURSE.

*T*hat's what can happen when you don't pay off your credit cards every month. Those high interest rates can make your debt grow as fast as weeds.

HOW DO YOU KNOW IF
YOU DON'T ASK?

There are no stupid questions. Don't be afraid to ask for a discount, question a charge, or any other related matter that concerns you. It's your money.

WE ALL DRIVE
USED CARS.

Within five minutes of getting behind the wheel of your new car, it's used. Same for your house, your clothes, everything you own. So before you spend money on something new, take a few minutes to think about how much you'll save by buying used.

A PENNY SAVED
IS A PENNY EARNED.

*N*eed we say more? Doris's mother often told her, "Take care of the pennies, and the dollars will take care of themselves."

WHY INVEST?

IF *WE* CAN DO IT,
YOU CAN TOO.

We are all just the lady next door, the average mother, the average grandmother. The fact that we live in a small town and have no special training seems to be an inspiration to others.

INVESTING IS AN EQUAL OPPORTUNITY.

Surveys have shown that 80 percent of women will need to take charge of their own finances at some point in their lives. More women are becoming involved with investing or retirement planning. Based on firsthand experience, we know that stocks offer both men and women, young and old, the same chance to expand their capital.

INVESTING IS AN
EDUCATION.

Our investment club is a means to learn. The $25 we pay in dues each month is our tuition for continuous learning about all types of investments.

INVESTMENT KNOWLEDGE
IS LIKE RETURN
ON EQUITY.

*I*t grows over time. We continue to have an education segment at every monthly meeting. Our investment knowledge keeps increasing as does the return on our investments.

YOU DON'T HAVE TO BET THE FARM TO MAKE HAY WHILE THE SUN SHINES.

There's a big difference between gambling and taking calculated risks, according to Carnell. Risk-taking can be a wise part of investing when knowledge and experience are used to help you manage.

MONEY CAN BEGET MONEY, AND ITS OFFSPRING CAN BEGET MORE.

Benjamin Franklin's special way of explaining compound interest makes just as much sense today.

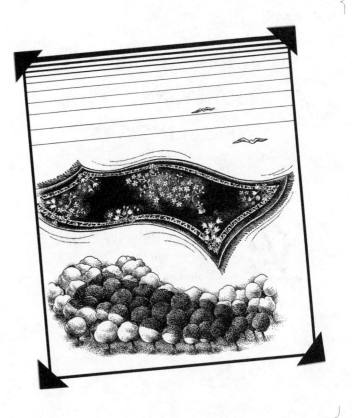

COMPOUND INTEREST IS
LIKE A MAGIC CARPET.

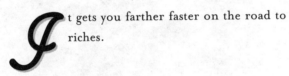 t gets you farther faster on the road to riches.

IT'S NOT HOW MUCH
MONEY YOU MAKE, IT'S
WHAT YOU DO WITH IT.

nn Corley's husband used to say this and we've always agreed. From stocks and bonds to mutual funds, when you consider all the choices we have these days, no matter how much or how little you start out with, there really is somewhere for everyone to invest.

THE TIME TO INVEST
FOR TOMORROW
IS YESTERDAY.

*I*t's never too soon to begin an investment program. We encourage our children and grandchildren to get started at an early age. The sooner you begin investing, the longer your money will be working for you. It will be there, having grown to larger figures, when you need it. But you must put some in today and every day.

OWNING STOCKS IS LIKE
RAISING CHILDREN.

You have to be patient and watch them grow. The end result should make you very proud.

WANT WHAT YOU HAVE,
HAVE WHAT YOU NEED.

nn Brewer likes to share what every woman needs: from birth to eighteen she needs good parents. From eighteen to thirty she needs good looks. From thirty to fifty she needs a good personality. But from fifty on, she had better have good investments!

LET YOUR GARDEN GROW.

*I*nvesting is like planting: You must choose the right seed; nurture it with a watchful eye; relax and let it grow to reap a bountiful harvest.

THE STOCK
MARKET

YOU DON'T WANT TO GET
MARRIED TO A STOCK.

When we get too attached to the stocks we follow, the decision to sell becomes more difficult. Deciding when to sell should be a business decision and not an emotional one.

WHEN IT COMES TO INVESTING, WE'RE ALL FUNDAMENTALISTS.

Experienced stock buyers rely either on *fundamentals* or *market timing*. Investing in fundamentals means looking for value inherent in a company and buying it to hold while that value grows. We are conservative investors with a long-term outlook. We expect stock prices to rise as value grows. We do not try to time the market.

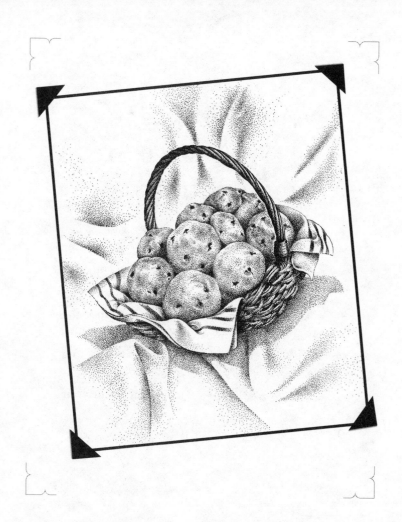

THE STOCK MARKET IS
LIKE SHIRLEY'S MUFFINS:
GUARANTEED TO RISE.

*T*he market's history of outstanding growth is undeniable when you look at its record since the beginning of the century. Stocks have plotted an overall upward trend, averaging an annual 9 percent return rate and outperforming most other investments. Have faith and remember: Even with all the dips, the market's general direction has been up!

WHEN THE
PARKING LOT'S FULL,
BUY THE STOCK.

One of our favorite stocks is Wal-Mart. We knew we were on to a good thing because when the Wal-Mart in Beardstown opened, the parking lot was full and people were coming out of the store with carts full of merchandise. So, watch the trends—see where people are buying and then do your homework!

DO YOUR
HOMEWORK.

*T*his is probably our most-quoted maxim: to invest wisely, you must study and learn as much as possible about individual companies. We use the information from Value Line Investment Advisory Service to complete NAIC's stock selection guide on each company to see if the fundamentals meet our expectations. If the current price is acceptable we will probably consider buying shares in the company. We apply this principle to everything we do: the more you know, the better off you are.

RESPECT YOUR BROKER, BUT DO YOUR OWN HOMEWORK.

Our stock broker, Homer, encourages us to do our homework. We never buy from a hot tip or just because Homer says it looks good. We do listen and promptly do our homework. If the fundamentals are favorable, we consider buying the company's stock.

IF YOU LIVE ON MAIN STREET YOU CAN STILL BEAT WALL STREET.

*I*n the first eleven years, our common-sense investment club averaged a 23.4 percent return on our money, better than nearly all Wall Street experts and a good bit better than the Standard & Poor's 500. All you need is the U.S. mail, a telephone, and the commitment to do your homework!

IF YOU LIKE KISSES,
TRY SOME HUGS.

One of Doris's favorite companies makes candy kisses. When the company started making hugs, she brought some to a meeting for all the members to enjoy. Following comments of approval of the new product their level of enthusiasm for the company increased. Personal insight about the product along with other available information serves a serious purpose.

STEADY
AS SHE GOES.

Dollar cost averaging is a stock purchase technique that requires you make regular purchases of a particular stock or set of stocks regardless of the market's level. Over an extended period of time during which stocks have moved both up and down, you will find that your average cost per share is lower than the average price for that period. The mathematical reason: You bought more shares when prices were low and fewer shares when prices were high.

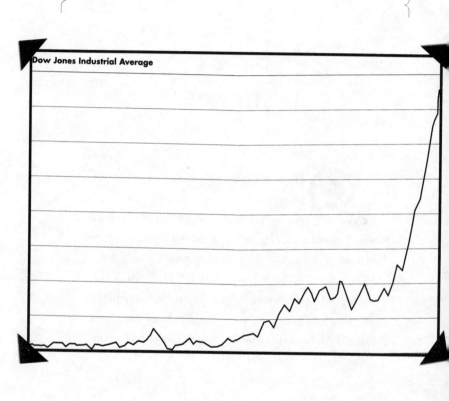

Dow Jones Industrial Average

WHEN THE DOW FALLS, IT'S TIME TO GO SHOPPING.

W hat goes down, must come up. It's contrary to intuition but it's been true of the stock market for 200 years. The trick is to remember this truism when stock prices plummet. The temptation for inexperienced investors is to get out as quickly as possible, to sell shares and take money back before its value diminishes any further. But more successful investors steel their nerves and buy as much stock as they can. We have even paid dues ahead of time to buy more stock when the market is down.

YOU DON'T HAVE
TO WEAR A THREE-PIECE
SUIT TO SUCCEED ON
WALL STREET.

*I*t doesn't matter if you live in the big city or on a farm in Beardstown—anyone, anywhere, can learn as much about investing in the stock market as those fancy "suits" on Wall Street.

IT PAYS TO KNOW THE
COMPANY YOU KEEP.

Carol says corporations are always willing to send their annual reports if you request them. Getting additional information may take a little more effort. If you want a stream of information, ask the investor relations department to put you on its mailing list.

MAXINE'S RECIPE FOR A SUCCESSFUL INVESTMENT CLUB: PREPARE THE FILLING AND MIX IN ONE LARGE STOCK POT.

Take one cup of awareness, two cups of willingness, one teaspoon knowledge, one tablespoon research, and one teaspoon of ability. Add a dollop of enthusiasm. Season with love, understanding, and patience. Simmer until all ingredients are well blended. Flavor improves over time.

PORTFOLIOS
AND ASSETS

THERE'S MORE TO
EGYPT THAN A
CAMEL RIDE.

We're talking about pyramids, of course. We use pyramid diagrams to visualize how our investments are distributed in terms of risk-reward ratios. We want the highest-risk investments at the top of the pyramid and the low-risk investments at the bottom, forming a broad, secure base.

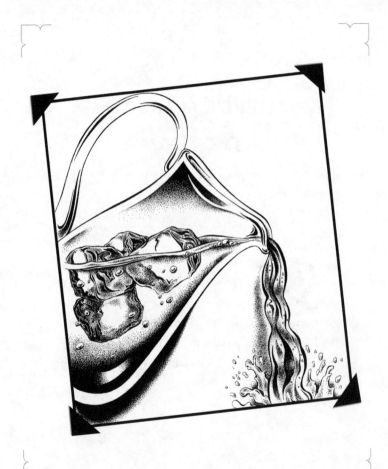

IF YOUR ASSETS ARE TOO LIQUID, YOU'RE POURING MONEY DOWN THE DRAIN.

That's because, in general, the more quickly you can turn an investment into cash (its liquidity), the less return on that investment you're likely to receive. Make sure you're not leaving any more of your money than necessary in such accounts or investments.

DON'T PUT ALL YOUR
EGGS IN ONE BASKET.

his is another way of saying we believe in diversification: the process of building a diverse investment portfolio, which includes different types of securities with different degrees of risk and maturity.

YOU CAN HAVE YOUR
PIE AND EAT IT TOO.

sset allocation is the division of money among various investment instruments. Think of it like a "pie" chart, with your investments representing different ingredients. An example might be 35 percent domestic stocks, 15 percent foreign stocks, 50 percent bonds. You can enjoy the rewards of your asset allocations once you determine what's best for you and invest in those "ingredients."

PIE CHARTS COME IN A VARIETY OF FLAVORS.

We chose "pies" to represent the asset allocations of various risk takers. The homemade apple pie represents the conservative investor, whose risk tolerance is low. Our lemon meringue pie represents the investor who is willing to take a little more risk, while the double Dutch chocolate cream pie has much more risky investments. You determine which pie is for you.

A PORTFOLIO IS MORE
THAN A BRIEFCASE.

*T*hat's not what Betty thought until six-
teen years ago. Now, of course, she
uses the term portfolio to refer to all
the securities held by an individual investor—or an
investment club.

IF YOU PLOW DIVIDENDS BACK INTO YOUR INVESTMENT SOIL, YOU'LL REAP A GREATER HARVEST.

When we receive dividend checks, we view them as fertilizer funds that will lead to a bigger yield of profit at some future harvest. We quickly plow them back into our portfolio. Automatically reinvesting your dividends is an excellent method of ensuring continued, steady investment growth over time. And you will be compounding your income because you will garner income from your initial investment and from the earnings on that investment itself.

130

TIME, NOT TIMING,
IS THE KEY.

Trying to time the market and moving in or out of certain assets based on short-term conditions is a surefire way to consistently underachieve. We think it's better to decide what asset allocation makes sense for you and invest for the long term.

DON'T KILL THE GOOSE
THAT'S LAYING GOLDEN
EGGS AFTER
THE FIRST EGG.

We don't sell after we have a profit if the potential for future growth exists. We like to reinvest our dividends and let that money continue to work for us.

PERFORMANCE, PERFORMANCE, PERFORMANCE.

When searching for a company to invest in we look at its historical past performance, consider the current performance, and estimate its future performance. If the numbers are good and the price is right we usually buy.

LOOK BEFORE
YOU LEAP.

*Y*ou wouldn't think of investing in the stock market without finding out as much as possible about the stock. You wouldn't send your child to a college you hadn't visited. Think of everything you buy as an investment. Look around, comparison shop, do your research.

OTHER KINDS
OF INVESTMENTS

EDUCATION IS AN INVESTMENT.

good education yields dividends for the rest of your life.

YOU HAVE TO *LET GO*
TO GROW.

Elsie had been afraid of investing because she didn't trust it. She felt if her money was in the bank, she'd be able to get hold of it right away. Now, says Elsie, "Instead of leaving it all in CDs and savings, I put some in mutual funds and ventured into the low-cost investment plan through National Association of Investors Corporation. I've really made use of my investment-club knowledge."

IF IT SEEMS
TOO GOOD TO BE TRUE,
IT USUALLY IS.

*I*n a perfect world, there would be an investment that provided a high rate of return with no risk of losing any money. Our world is far from perfect.

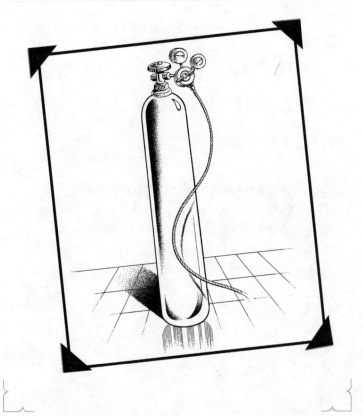

YOUR IRA MAY BE
YOUR LIFE SUPPORT.

We believe IRAs, SEPs, Keoghs, 401k's, and all the other tax-deferred investment plans will save you tax dollars now and grow to keep you comfortable in your retirement.

OUT OF SIGHT,
OUT OF MIND.

Automatic payroll deductions are a nest builder. Carol has money taken directly out of her paycheck from the insurance company where she works and has it invested in an annuity. She says, "If I don't have it, I don't miss it. It goes to the annuity and it just keeps growing."

THE RIGHT MATH CAN
SAVE YOU MONEY.

*B*uffy feels that the biweekly mortgage plan is the best bargain around. On a $55,000 mortgage at 8 percent interest, the monthly payment is about $404. If you pay half, or $202, every two weeks, you will save over $26,000 in interest over the life of the loan. It's the most painless way we know to save that kind of money. And the savings increase on larger mortgages or higher rates of interest.

THERE IS A
MUTUAL FUND
FOR EVERYONE.

*T*oday you can find mutual funds for all types of investments. It's a way to get instant diversification. Just as we use Value Line to find information about stocks, we use Morningstar to evaluate our mutual fund choices.

WHEN OPPORTUNITY KNOCKS BE THE FIRST AT THE DOOR.

We often hear people say, "If only I had done that." We believe in acting on our opportunities and encourage you to do the same.

MANY
HAPPY
RETURNS

THERE ARE NO GUARANTEES IN THE BOOK OF LIFE.

r in the book value of stocks. Be patient and you'll be rewarded.

REMEMBER THE
ROOT BEER.

Carnell and her young daughter were driving a new car home when her daughter asked if they could stop and get a root beer. Carnell told her, "I don't have any money, do you have any money?" Her daughter said, "No, I don't have any money. Are you telling me that you have enough money for a new car, but not a nickel for a root beer?" Lest we get too caught up in saving big money at the risk of sacrificing life's small pleasures, Carnell says, "Remember that it's important to have those nickels for a root beer, too."

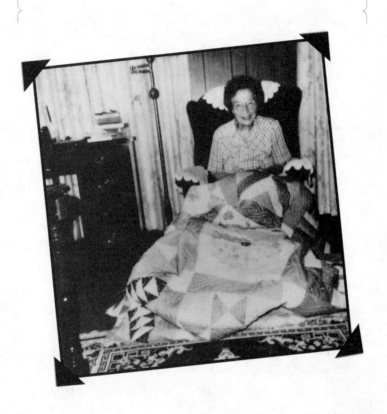

DON'T BUILD
A NEST EGG AND THEN
SIT IN A TREE!

The whole reason for having enough money is to enjoy life and to be able to give something back to others. From sewing quilts to making meals, from collecting glass to writing letters, we try to make the most of our time. In the process, we have a lot of fun. We hope you will start growing your own nest egg—and that you will make time for whatever makes life worthwhile for you.

REACH OUT TO CATCH
THE BRASS RING.

*R*uth encourages everyone to take advantage of the opportunities that come their way no matter what their age. She fulfilled her fantasy when Phil Donahue invited the investment club to New York City to tape his show. The vision of New York at Christmastime still lingers in her memories.

LIFE'S BEST LAID PLANS OFTEN GO ASTRAY.

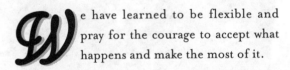e have learned to be flexible and pray for the courage to accept what happens and make the most of it.

BLESS OUR
COMPUTERS.

*I*sn't it great to be able to change your mind or make those corrections without starting over? Sure saves on the paper and on our time.

LIFE IS FULL
OF CHOICES.

The Lord gave us minds to make decisions. Let's make good ones!

IF YOU CAN'T AFFORD CHAMPAGNE, ENJOY GINGER ALE.

Margaret reminds us to live within our means. When planning a daughter's wedding, for example, this is important to remember. You can be creative and still have a beautiful wedding. Tomorrow does come, and you do not want to be mired in debt.

INVESTMENTS ARE A MEANS TO AN END, NOT AN END IN THEMSELVES.

Try to keep your perspective when you monitor your investing progress. Hazel encourages us to stop and smell the roses. She knows the joy of relaxing and enjoying every day to its fullest.

IT'S NOT WHETHER WE WIN OR LOSE, IT'S HOW WE PLAY THE GAME.

We've made our fair share of investing mistakes. But for every loss we've taken in the stock market, we've gained invaluable knowledge for our next investment.

YOU CAN'T BUY LOVE,
BUT YOU CAN
INVEST IN IT.

*Y*ou don't have to spend a lot of money to entertain your children or grandchildren—play with them instead. It's a lot more fun, and the memories you create will last a lifetime.

THE SHORTEST DISTANCE
BETWEEN TWO PEOPLE
IS A SMILE.

It takes almost twice as many facial muscles to frown as it takes to smile. We like to be efficient, so we'd rather smile than frown.

THE THREE THINGS THAT
MAKE LIFE WORTH LIVING
ARE SOMETHING TO DO,
SOMEONE TO LOVE, AND
SOMETHING TO HOPE FOR.

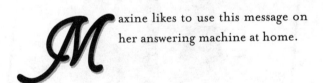

Maxine likes to use this message on her answering machine at home.

PRAYER IS THE BEST
INVESTMENT OF ALL.

"Everything has gone so well for us," Betty says. "We're certain the Man upstairs has had a lot to do with it." At every monthly meeting we pause to thank Him for our many blessings.

The Beardstown Ladies are fourteen women who are members of an investment club that was established fourteen years ago. They live in or near Beardstown, Illinois, and still hold regular meetings on the first Thursday of every month. They are the authors of three best-selling books, *The Beardstown Ladies' Common-Sense Investment Guide, The Beardstown Ladies' Stitch-in-Time Guide to Growing Your Nest Egg,* and *The Beardstown Ladies' Guide to Smart Spending for Big Savings.*

Robin Dellabough is associate publisher at Seth Godin Productions. A former freelance writer, she has worked on more than a dozen books, including *The Beardstown Ladies' Stitch-in-Time Guide to Growing Your Nest Egg,* and *The Beardstown Ladies' Guide to Smart Spending for Big Savings.*

Seth Godin Productions creates books in Irvington-on-Hudson, New York. To date, it has more than 90 titles in print, including works on business, celebrities, computers, and more.

NOW YOU CAN OWN THE ORIGINAL VIDEO!

COOKIN' UP PROFITS ON WALL STREET

A GUIDE TO COMMON-SENSE INVESTING

with

THE BEARDSTOWN LADIES

Shot on location in Beardstown, Illinois, this one-hour video gives you the flavor and spirit of the Ladies "up close and personal." The Beardstown Ladies' award-winning videotape *Cookin' Up Profits on Wall Street* tells you everything you need to know to create your own common sense financial plan, organize and run your own investment club, and look for companies using the same fundamentals the Ladies use.

CALL 1-800-359-3276 TO ORDER. ONLY $19.95!

MasterCard, Visa, or Discover accepted.
Or use the coupon below for check or money order.

- -

NAME: _____

ADDRESS: _____

CITY: _____ STATE: _____ ZIP: _____

YES! Please rush me _____ VHS copies of *Cookin' Up Profits on Wall Street*
at $19.95 plus $4.95 shipping and handling each.
(Illinois residents please add sales tax at 6.25%.)

I have enclosed my check or money order for _____

MAIL TO: CENTRAL PICTURE ENTERTAINMENT, INC. VIDEO ORDER DEPARTMENT
P.O. BOX 578-219, CHICAGO, ILLINOIS 60657-8219

Please allow 6-8 weeks for delivery.